digging

smiling

hugging

sweeping

bouncing

stamping

reading

crawling

sucking

# For Jack

First published 1993 by Walker Books Ltd
87 Vauxhall Walk, London SE11 5HJ

© 1993 Shirley Hughes
This book has been typeset in Plantin Light.

Printed and bound in Hong Kong
by Dai Nippon Printing Co. (H.K.) Ltd

British Library Cataloguing in Publication Data
A catalogue record for this book is available from the British Library.

ISBN 0-7445-2513-6

# Bouncing

## Shirley Hughes

WALKER BOOKS
LONDON

When I throw my big shiny ball...

it bounces away from me.

Bounce, bounce, bounce, bounce!

Then it rolls along the ground, then it stops.

I like bouncing too. In the mornings
I bounce on my bed,

and the baby bounces in his cot.

Mum and Dad's big bed is an even better place to bounce.

But Dad doesn't much like being bounced
on in the early morning.

So we roll on the floor instead, and the
baby bounces on ME!

After breakfast he
does some dancing
in his baby-bouncer,

and I do some dancing
to the radio.

At my play-group there are big cushions on
the floor where lots of children
can bounce together.

And at home there's a big sofa where we can bounce when Mum isn't looking.

Grandpa and I know a good bouncing game.

I ride on his knees and we sing:

This is the way the ladies ride: trit-trot, trit-trot;

This is the way the gentlemen ride: tarran, tarran;

This is the way the farmers ride: clip-clop, clip-clop;

This is the way the jockeys ride: gallopy, gallopy,

and FALL OFF!

I like bouncing.

I bounce about all day...

bounce, bounce,
bounce, bounce!

Until in the end I stop bouncing,

and go off to sleep.

running

painting

looking

drinking

bouncing

counting

sitting

bending

scowling